PARABLES

FROM JESUS
Book 1

Deadra Neary

WestBow Press books may be ordered through booksellers or by contacting:

WestBow Press
A Division of Thomas Nelson & Zondervan
1663 Liberty Drive
Bloomington, IN 47403
www.westbowpress.com
844-714-3454

Because of the dynamic nature of the Internet, any web addresses or links contained in this book may have changed since publication and may no longer be valid. The views expressed in this work are solely those of the author and do not necessarily reflect the views of the publisher, and the publisher hereby disclaims any responsibility for them.

Any people depicted in stock imagery provided by Getty Images are models, and such images are being used for illustrative purposes only.
Certain stock imagery © Getty Images.

ISBN: 978-1-6642-9841-5 (sc)
ISBN: 978-1-6642-9843-9 (hc)
ISBN: 978-1-6642-9842-2 (e)

Library of Congress Control Number: 2023907645

Print information available on the last page.

WestBow Press rev. date: 05/02/2023

WESTBOW
PRESS®
A DIVISION OF THOMAS NELSON
& ZONDERVAN

You Are a Light - Matthew 5:14-16
The Speck and the Log - Matthew 7:1-5
Wise Man and the Foolish Man - Matthew 7:24-27

Dedication

This book is dedicated to Jesus Christ, my Lord, who gave me the inspiration and ability to write these poems. To my loving husband, Kevin, who has supported, encouraged, and proofed every word. To great-nephew Bradley Smith, the motivator for this book.

par . a . ble

A parable is a story Jesus told for me,
teaching me how my life should be.
His stories will help me grow up strong and wise,
so I can see things through His godly eyes.
To understand His mercy, love, and grace,
and know for sure I will see His face.

So read with me these stories so true,
from Jesus, our Savior, to me and to you.
You Are a Light - Matthew 5:14-16
You are a light for all to see,
the Savior's love for you and me.

A town on a hill will always be seen,
so let your light shine, oh, let it gleam.

Don't hide your light or tuck it away,
the darkness makes some people afraid.

Let it shine from here to there,
oh let it shine everywhere.
Let it shine on the mountain high,
let it shine throughout the sky.
Let it shine through the valley at night,
it will be such a beautiful sight.

Your light will bring such wonderful joy,
happiness, and peace to each girl and boy.

Don't hide your light, oh let it shine,
so others will see our Savior divine.

Par – a – ble

A parable is a story Jesus told for me,
teaching me how my life shall be.
This story shows God loves us all the same,
when we find fault in others it's just a shame.
You have faults just like others do,
and Jesus loves them and He loves you.
So read with me this story so true,
from Jesus, our Savior, to me and to you.

The Speck and the Log - Matthew 7:1-5
The lesson of this story shall be,
we all have sin in our life you see.
So do not judge or you'll be judged too,
the way you judge will come back to you.

You cannot see the speck in someone's eye,
because the log in yours is big and wide.
Get rid of your log, your sin if you please,
then you can see how to help those in need.

Par – a – ble

A parable is a story Jesus told for me,
teaching me how my life shall be.
This story teaches us to trust God in all that you do.
His love and protection will cover you.
Do what is right and be assured,
your home in Heaven is now secured.
So read with me this story so true,
from Jesus, our Savior, to me and to you.

Wise Man and the Foolish Man - Matthew 7:24-27
Whoever hears and obeys these teachings of mine,
his earthly life will turn out just fine.

One will be foolish and one will be wise.
One will be happy and the other will cry.
God's teaching is firm and will not give way,
like building a house that is here to stay.

The rains came and the wind blew,
the wise man knew just what to do.
He trusted in God and had great faith.
From Satan's snares he knew he was safe.

24

The foolish man does not listen or obey.
He is in danger of becoming Satan's prey.
The rains came and the wind blew,
but the foolish man did not know what to do.
The house he built will not stand,
because it is built on shifting sand.

So listen and learn, trust and obey,
and know God is with you every day.

Printed in the United States
by Baker & Taylor Publisher Services